*Jeremiah,*

# OHIO

# Jeremiah,
# OHIO

*a novel in poems*

*Adam Sol*

ANANSI

This edition published in 2008 by
House of Anansi Press Inc.
110 Spadina Avenue, Suite 801
Toronto, ON, M5V 2K4
Tel. 416-363-4343
Fax 416-363-1017
www.anansi.ca

Distributed in Canada by
HarperCollins Canada Ltd.
1995 Markham Road
Scarborough, ON, M1V 5M8
Toll free tel. 1-800-387-0117

Distributed in the United States by
Publishers Group West
1700 Fourth Street
Berkeley, CA 94710
Toll free tel. 1-800-788-3123

House of Anansi Press is committed to protecting our natural environment.
As part of our efforts, this book is printed on paper that contains 100%
post-consumer recycled fibres, is acid-free, and is processed chlorine-free.

12 11 10 09 08    1 2 3 4 5

LIBRARY AND ARCHIVES CANADA CATALOGUING IN PUBLICATION DATA

Sol, Adam, 1969–
Jeremiah, Ohio / Adam Sol.

Poems.

ISBN 978-0-88784-791-2

1. Jeremiah (Biblical prophet) — Poetry.  I. Title.

PS8587.O41815J47 2008      C811'.6      C2008-901231-3

Library of Congress Control Number: 2008922791

Cover design: Bill Douglas
Typesetting: Laura Brady

Canada Council    Conseil des Arts    ONTARIO ARTS COUNCIL
for the Arts      du Canada           CONSEIL DES ARTS DE L'ONTARIO

We acknowledge for their financial support of our publishing program the Canada Council
for the Arts, the Ontario Arts Council, and the Government of Canada through the Book
Publishing Industry Development Program (BPIDP).

Printed and bound in Canada

CONTENTS

Invocation | 1

Essen | 2

Chillicothe Was the First Capital of the Ohio Territory | 4

At the Flea Market | 6

16% of Peebles Residents Report German Ancestry | 8

Song of Sixty Days | 10

Communion at Bruce's Apartment | 12

Confession During the Failing Buzz of
the Post-Game Wrap-Up | 13

Three Months Earlier | 16

Jeremiah at the Outlet Mall | 17

Athens Has Been Called One of the Top Ten
Most Haunted Places in America | 19

Lament for the Girls of Mt. Gilead | 21

Modus Operandi | 23

Stephen Hibbs at the Snell Street Luncheonette | 26

Tutorial at the Corner of Wolfpen and 143 | 27

Driving Past a Broken Down Pickup Full of
Migrants Late for Work in Willard | 28

Due to Lighted Arches on High Street, Columbus Was, for a Time, Known as the Most Brilliantly Lit City in the Country | 29

Doom Again on U.S. 36 | 32

Ohio Portrait in 5-Syllable Road Signs | 34

Right Lane Must Exit | 35

Elegy for the Truck | 36

Ashland Radio | 38

Aftermath | 39

Waking and Hearing the Call of the City | 40

Slopping in the Rain Between Wadsworth and Poe | 42

Akron's History Is Colorful, Painful, Diverse, and Inspiring | 44

Bullfrog Jeremiah | 45

Jeremiah's Wounds | 46

Jeremiah at the All Saints Cathedral, Youngstown | 47

Jeremiah Plays Chess | 49

What I've Got So Far, Approaching Youngstown and September | 50

Hitching a Ride Out of California, PA | 52

Swedish Immigrant Carl Eric Wickman Began Transporting Miners from Hibbing to Alice, MN, in 1914 | 54

Ponderosa Confession | 57

Villanelle for Jeremiah's Son | 58

Jeremiah, PA | 60

Pay When Boarding | 62

Psalm of Scranton | 64

Jeremiah Defaces a Roadside Shrine | 65

Jeremiah at Beis T'fillah of Teaneck | 66

Jeremiah's Blues on the GW Bridge | 68

Manhattanville Expansion Raises Questions About Aesthetics | 70

Church of the Intercession | 71

Hananiah | 73

Redemption of the Field at Broadway and 88th | 74

Gentrification of Upper Manhattan Is Not Yet Complete | 75

At the Converted Bank | 76

Our People. Our Work. Our Values. | 78

Sprinting Through the 60s | 80

Quickly Find Our Upcoming Events | 81

Acrostic Lament | 83

Come Spend a Great Day Downtown | 84

Declaiming from the Wreckage | 86

Post No Bills | 88

Sgt. Ebediah ("Eddie") King | 89

Incidental Music Is Often Background Music | 90

Fingerprinting | 92

Song of Repentance | 94

Support the International Brotherhood of
Electrical Workers | 95

In the Holding Pen | 96

Religious Song | 98

Items in the Prisoner's Possession | 99

Emotionally Disturbed Persons May Be Released into the
Custody of Family Members at the Discretion of the
Commanding Officer | 100

We're On Our Way | 102

Newark Local | 103

Forty-Two Percent of Greyhound Passengers Are
Between the Ages of 18 and 34 | 105

How I wanted to see a vision then | 107

Last Words | 108

Song of Leaving | 109

Acknowledgments | 111

These are the words of Jeremiah, the son of Hank,
    of the failed farmers and short-order cooks
    who tilled and tore the soil of Southern Ohio
        in the days that became years that became confusion.

These are his words, poor bastard,
    who roared himself ragged
        during the reign of Soandso and his Valiant Pals.

Hear the summons, o wanderers and worriers!
    See me pulling the planks from your porch!

Woe unto ye, corporate communicators!
    Behold the oily ends of your extended lunches!

Yea, I have been sent to root out and pull down,
    to lubricate and decimate,
        to build and to plant.

Who will accompany me on my trail of frustration?
    Who will lend me a button?

I have seen and will give voice to my grief.
    I will be delivered C.O.D.

May the words of my mouth
        and the declamations of my fury
    tear holes in the outerwear of the people.

Let them feel the hot gust.

Begin with the wind disguising itself as a rake. An exit sign points out toward the saddest patch of grass in Western Ohio. A man has heard grave announcements from passing radios and resigned himself to a night of wet gravel. He can smell an ambient summer storm gathering its skirts like an expectant mother, and has reasons to expect the worst: his lost sweater, or the thigh bruises given him by an overzealous camera salesman.

There have been hours of walking and hours of standing still. And his cardboard plea for Columbus may as well read Belgium.

A blue Buick Skylark pulls onto the median from the opposing lane, as if to let the man know he hasn't gone unseen in the shrill heat. Hitching his greasepants the man considers an idea of communion, and hopsteps across the empty asphalt toward her chariot. But by the time he has crossed the divide the woman at the wheel has lobbed a paper bag through her window into the hissing milkweed and torn off, shredding roadside wildgrass with her magnificent radials.

When he looks back west with the package in his fist to offer a gesture of thanks or greeting, she has diminished into a mere blur on the slope, rising then winking out like a last glimpse of the old life he once lived in a town with flax fields and homemade honey.

Inside the bag: a napkin to wipe his bleeding ear. A plastic spoon to dig for snails. An apple. And printed words wrapped jauntily around a tub of yoghurt: "70% LESS FAT" glorious on the still-cool container in his grip.

The man sits to work his mouth around the rush of unlikely letters embracing his hammered hand, and contemplates the need for some significant gesture. Another semi wrongs its horn blasting past in a flurry of dust and shattered grasshoppers. The man hoists his tub in furious salute: "I receive your Pectin! I receive your Xanthan Gum!" chewing the syllables, nourished enough to knot his knees toward Richwood.

*CHILLICOTHE WAS THE FIRST CAPITAL OF*
*THE OHIO TERRITORY*


It's two, and once I've dropped off
my load of loaves and Twinkies
at the State Pen In-And-Out,
I can spend the afternoon
smoking at the Indian
Mount State Park. Dispatch doesn't
need the van till five thirty,
and each cigarette burns off
a little of the day's shame.
No one's looking for me here.

But halfway through my first fire
I hear a man at the gate
standing with his arms outspread
like he is trying to call
down the rain. He is making
roaring noises in his throat
and when the ranger asks him
to move along, he starts
yelling, "What unrighteousness
have your fathers found in me
that now they are gone from me?!"
Something like that. The ranger
is just a kid, probably
working off student loans, so
I say, "Listen, buddy, d'you
need a ride or what?" Right away
he grabs his army duffel
and slings it into my truck.

He sits on the floor in back
next to a crate of Sno-Balls.
Then he asks, "What is thy name?"
I can hardly keep myself
from laughing, but I answer,
"Bruce Gray, scholar and bread man."
Jeremiah shakes my hand,
and looks straight into my face.
His hands are already scarred
and yellow with calluses.
"Are you upright and holy?"
"Sure." "Can you transcribe the words
I speak?" "I can type, if that's
what you mean." "Good. I thank you
for your kindness. It will not
go unnoticed, if you catch
my drift." "I catch it." "Drive on."

*AT THE FLEA MARKET*


All along the riverside my towns are breaking down.
     My Delhis and Mount Orabs,
     my New Harmonys and Crowns.

I lost my heart at Dairy Mart for lack of home-baked bread,
     and blundered into wonder
     and was crushed like a possum on Route 32.

Will you hear, O my people? Will you heed my bells and whistles?
Will you teen girls worrying your split ends
     remark on my resonance and tears?
         Where can I go to find solace,

if even the restrooms are for customers only? Yea,

the women of Williamsburg
     are selling suitcases at the Sunday jubilee,
     along with ceramic geese and rifles.

What can they learn from me, except that their villages
  are vanishing?
     Behold, they are sitting on a bowl that has
been dropped from the table. Like a potter's toy
     we must be refired.

They know this well. Their town is an astonishment and a hissing.
They should know better than to recline on lawn chairs
     and bake their bellies like berries.

O fair-haired mothers! O mole-chinned grannies!

Remove your orange sunglasses —
    reveal the squinting of your hearts!
Be not worse than your uncles who sowed wheat
    and reaped thorns in this asphalt pasture!

Save your old yards with their hopeful black-eyed susans
    and their weary black-eyed Susans.

Way back before his heart broke
I suppose Jeremiah
was just as crazy as all
his neighbors. But that was long
before I met him. By then
he'd been seen cursing dumpsters
in Lynchburg, scolding billboards
and McDonald's customers
even as far as Peebles.

As for me, I'd been feeling
embarrassed, knowing full well
that even my loneliness
was common, that my profound
despair was a tired cliché.
I'd dropped out of grad school and
disappointed my mentors,
because I can't see myself
fitting into the role of
Expert in Po Mo Flim Flam.
If only I could yadda
yadda instead of blahblahblah.
And then, to top it all off,
I fucked up the closest thing
I'd had to a family
since I left my sad mother
to her lists and memories.
I was in purgatory,
delivering faux-baked goods
to gas station groceries,

mini-marts, and convenience
stores in Southern Ohio
from Athens to Columbus.

Of course I thought he was nuts,
in a harmless hobo way,
and when I gave him a box
of Ho Hos, he nearly cried
from gratitude. It had been
a long while since I had done
something good for anyone.

So I invited him home
for a shower, an old pair
of pants, dinner, and a couch.
Why he made the decision
to promote me from chauffeur
to secretary and aide
is a mystery to me.
Maybe because I said Yes.
The "Baked" painted on the side
of my cab had been scraped off
by some bored schoolboys in Clark,
so the side of the truck just
said, "Goods." That, too, may have been
enough, desperate as he was
for signs that the world had not
completely abandoned him.

*SONG OF SIXTY DAYS*

It is true I went to see the Mayor
      in his office of plaques.

And true he showed me photos of himself
      with notables local and spectacular.

True too that though I held his elbow and begged him
      to abandon the chase and submit to his fate,

to kowtow to the clowns for the sake of the town,

he held his haughty head high
      and frowned.

The man is in the full sway of hand-sets,
      biceps and fudge,
      and though he nodded,

his very chin was not his own.

Sixty days I have wandered these hills,
      and I have seen little to lighten my heart.

Tables are still set without trembling,
      and salesmen thumb scales from Damascus to Defiance.

When will my people learn
      that their china is made of their own bones?

Who will tell them that their city was doomed
        from the start to test products and poisons?

Why have they cast aside my teachings,
        and erected rapacious billboards
                like so many weeds in the fields?

Yea, they are a city of cash cows.

They will be slaughtered for cut-rate soup stock,
        and their labels will shout judgment

from the shelves of mini-marts
        from Waco to Tungsten.

Two men on a cracked couch, shiny with pizza grease and the inarticulate reflection of the Reds in a close one against the Cardinals. The silent understanding of passing over another bottle of Bud. And the resonant syllogisms over the health of Griffey's shoulder. It's going to be a long summer. J exhausted from baring his head and chest to the winds and passersby of Chillicothe. B too glib to understand himself — his words make sense, but they aren't true. Boone hits a lonely two-out double off the right field wall. It amounts to nothing — Dunn whiffs in three pitches. There is a small spiritual truth in their shared sadness and frustration. Is this enough? Tonight it is enough.

CONFESSION DURING THE FAILING BUZZ OF THE
POST-GAME WRAP-UP

*I lied earlier. I'm not upright or holy.*

I turned the volume down, and we watched Joe Morgan
equivocating with his eyebrows.

All are holy in the eyes of —
*Well, not upright, then.*
How have you slouched?

There was a touch of glee in his voice, as if he'd been waiting all
night for me to speak. Or as if I had something stuck to my nose.

*I feel as if I'm in the process of failing as a person.*

The smirk disappeared then, and he turned to me. His eyebrows
turned up, and he was listening with a strange, blunt attention.
Who had I ever talked to like this?

*First off, I sort of got between my best friends' marriage.*

The commercials were loud, even with the sound off. Each frame
cut flashed and glittered until the tv strobed. J leaned back and
rubbed his grizzled chin.

I see. And you seek redemption.
*I guess.*
From your God.
*I don't know about that.*

He stood up and unbuttoned his shirt, draping it over the screen. Underneath was a faded black T-shirt that said Caleb's Grill.

> Listen, young man, if you want redemption from your
> friends, ask your friends. Please tell me we didn't find each
> other so that I might ask your friends to redeem you.
> *All right, then. From my god. Whoever that is.*

He held up his finger, and the glimmer was back.

> The man who knows not his God
>         is like the man who cannot see his intestine.
> *Huh?*
> No one can see it, you dope. But we all know when
>         it's upset with us.

He even smiled then, with a preacher's satisfaction. But when he saw that I wasn't laughing he cleared his throat and started shouting at the walls.

> Pity on the widows and orphans!
>         Mercy for the sad and alone!

> We have here a boy who has broken his father's window,
>         and is confused by the silence.

> From whom must he seek expiation?
>         Which local spigot will spout something holy for him
>                 to cleanse himself of sin?
> Where is the sound and the slurry?

My neighbor banged once on the wall, so he leaned in close, so that I could smell the anchovies on his breath. He put his hand on my head and closed his eyes.

Don't worry, my boy. Daddy's not mad at you.

Maybe it was the beer, but as I lolled off to my frameless bed I thought, Holy shit, I've got to hear more of this. Then his head appeared in my doorway, framed in shadow behind the hallway light.

Tomorrow you will drive me to the Outlandish Mall.
We'll see what you have that's redeemable.

Bruce, fuzz-headed, trundles to the toilet during half-convincing commercials, pot-vodka shimmer all over the room. The swirl of hallway poster art and sticky rented carpet dust only adds to the spell, Beth and Tony behind on the couch, hands loosely mingled on her knee. A majestic voice calls for an end to the plague of plaque, and Bruce is in love with everything — with Tony's apartment, with television drama as a developing art form open to critical analysis, with Tony's post-structuralist insights, with Beth's smart wit, with his life on his own with friends he admires, Beth's overlong canine teeth, Tony's hyperbolic glasses. As his gut relieves itself of the evening's early drinks, he sees the hominess of their cramped quarters with a kind of religious awe: toothpaste and mascara, Clearasil and Tampax all contributing to an ideal of partnership and balance that he had never before understood. And there, on an eyelevel, soap-smeared shelf, is her hairbrush. As he washes his hands, he leans closer, squinting and joyous. He dries, thoroughly, and with a ceremonial grace picks up the object with the central fingers of both hands. Bringing the object closer to his face, he deeply inhales, ecstatic with the lush smell of shampoo, of hair, of something vaguely burnt, of the intimate and the loved. At that moment the door creaks open and Beth's stunned face appears in the medicine cabinet mirror. Luckily, the words are already tumbling out of her mouth: "You okay? We thought you might have passed out." But by the end of the sentence, her composure has collapsed, and she backs into the couch, comically gape-mouthed. Tony has something to say about the *Seinfeld* rerun they are watching, but it is lost in their strange new secret. Bruce returns to his perpendicular love seat, aware of her stare.

## JEREMIAH AT THE OUTLET MALL

Even the parking lot is a three day walk across,
    where a man named Harold Hillman
    has painted his initials around the shadows of the cars.
    HHHHHHHHHHHH

Behold! Only he has left his mark on this wilderness.
All else is asphalt and fiberglass.

Behold the pyramid of linens!
Behold the bushel of spoons!
    Yea, I have not seen such riches since yesterday.

How can we know ourselves in this concrete cookie sheet?
    The East is the same as the West.
    The North is the same as Sheol.

I care not for your discount clearance sale, says the Lord.
I scoff at your makeshift markdowns.

Show me the hand that wove the fiber
    and I will bless you and your auction house.

Introduce me to the underdressed pressers,
    and to the boys who stick pins in shirts
    while waiting for their overdue mothers.

Who will appease them? Where will they park?

Their lot will not be evenly delineated,
    nor will it contain lamppost night lighting,

yet I believe we will see their glory at our feet,
     and around our necks,
          before this paved plain gives birth to righteousness.

*ATHENS HAS BEEN CALLED ONE OF THE TOP TEN*
*MOST HAUNTED PLACES IN AMERICA*


Once we got to the mall
            I had a decision
        to make: to ditch or stick.

I sat down on the curb
            while J started to preach,
        working up a good sweat
            between the minivans.

He was spectacular,
        calling and gesturing,
            chasing the terrified
        shoppers and employees
from the air-conditioned
        stores to their baking cars.

Half the time I couldn't
            hear what he was saying,
        but when I could I was
drawn to his certainty,
        or at least his passion.

        Was he really a man
        of God? Could he somehow
            absolve my sorry self

of whatever had brought
        me here in the first place?

It seemed much more likely
        than driving a bread van.

When he was finished he
            ambled over — surprised,
        I think, that I was still there.

I said, Where to next, boss?
            He paused for a second,
        nodding, then kicked my shoe.

He said, You'll need to pack
        some extra socks and things.

Back at my apartment
            I put shirts in a bag
        while J ransacked cupboards
            for canned goods and dried fruit.

My one concern was for
        the truck. It wasn't mine.

And the poor old clunker
        wouldn't last past Ashland.

*LAMENT FOR THE GIRLS OF MT. GILEAD*

They are gone over the state line —
       to Muncie, to Gary, to Terre Haute.

And their mothers,
       who used to play Pete Seeger on phonographs,
       and would wonder at wonders,

are bent over kitchen tables now,
cheeks creased by the heels of their hands.
       Their summer dresses fray and their teeth clench tight,

for their city has been abandoned by its only hope.
How they sit, solitary,
       and refuse to be comforted,

even by the riches
       that flicker by on banners and billboards. O!

I have brought my hands to my face
       and felt only paper!
I have struck a fist to my knee and could not reflect.

Long ago I was banished from the city on the hill
       by the bloated brother of a pleasure boatman,

and yet I still believe in the gold,
       and in the passages of brittle fingers.

See how the water tower sways like a palm in a storm!

It is there, inside that iron cavern,
    where I shall sleep tonight,
        for like it I am hollow and dry with rust.

I am balanced on stilts, and a sneeze
    could send me reeling.

Why must I break my brain in this way?
Why must I sing a song of calamity
    when I would rather play clarinet for retirees?

Lord, I would give my right ear
    for a well-wetted reed.

*MODUS OPERANDI*

In the beginning,
in the towns he knew,
        he'd have a specific place in mind.

But as we moved east
and further from home
        he would start murmuring in the cab

when he'd seen a spot
that needed a good
        talking-to. Donut shops, gas stations,

where the loud displays
clashed with the postures
        of the women behind the counters.

The boxes of cakes
didn't last as long
        as I thought they would when we left home.

I interpreted
Jeremiah's rants
        as half-politics, half-religion,

but what compelled me
was their warped music,
        something necessary and unique.

I would pull over
and just let him go.
        In those first weeks it was almost like

I was dropping off
my father for his
        regular game of canasta with

his old war buddies —
it was that casual.
        After, he'd collect his clothes and hop

back into the truck
humming, still buzzing
        with the words, and the response he got.

He'd wipe the spit off,
and we'd ride away
        with the laughter and the dismissals

trailing behind us
like a kind of ex-
        haust, half-believing we'd done some good.

Occasionally
the police would get
        involved in running us out of town,

but usually we
weren't around long
        enough to attract much attention.

Once I got the hang
of his time-table
          I'd take the opportunity

to pick up groceries
or gather my notes.
          By June I'd filled seven legal pads

full of his speeches
but still didn't know
          what he wanted me to do with them.

At night, by firelight,
he would read his day,
          grunting. Sometimes he would scratch things out.

I realize now
that he was forming
          his philosophy as we traveled

(or receiving it),
in preparation
          for what would happen to him later.

I was halfway through my third helping of all-you-can-eat
hashbrowns, tinkering with the idea of saying something stupid to
Edith the pug-nosed waitress but knowing I was better off just
clattering my fork when I wanted another plateful. Then in he
walks like something out of a comic book. I could smell his burnt
beard, and the way his hands shook I thought at first he needed a
fix. I've been there. So I got up to give him a buck for coffee anyway,
and he turns to me and says — I'm not fooling here, he says, "My
bowels writhe for want of oil." Call me crazy, but I thought he
meant the hashbrowns — they were oily enough — but when
I turned to fetch my plate Edith had already cleared it, thinking I
was up to pay my check. The man passed me with a belch and said
something to the busboy about trimming his sideburns. I think
if he had stood on the counter and proclaimed that he was Elvis
reincarnated to redeem the world, I would have believed, dropped
my keys, and followed him. It wasn't his prophetic hair, his
collapsed sandals, or that look of shock that movies always tell
us means a brush with death — it was his hoarse voice, which
reminded me of some teacher I must have had when I was young
and full of promise. I know I've heard that voice before, and I'm
sure I'd remember if I heard it again which makes me sorry I paid
my tab, over-tipped Edith, and pushed myself through the shatter-
proof door before he spoke again.

Bloated with blisters, Bruce roughly rubs his rump,

curses his cracks and creases, sweatily swears to himself

that folly has foundered him — this trip is trash.

Jeremiah, jaunty and fresh, fingers a follicle

and sniffs the sultry smell of nearby nourishment.

"We work well together! Tomorrow or Tuesday

let's let loose in bigger, better boroughs.

The more men we meet, the more likely some will listen."

But Bruce is bitter. "No one even came near

to hear your hollering. They ran across the road

to avoid your vain voice. They didn't dare

come close in curiosity. They fled like flies!"

"Yes, yes. They yearn, but they're yellow. I'm tasked to teach them

how to handle honesty in words of wild wonder.

Slowly the message will seep into their masticating minds.

Fear not for the fleeing friend, or even the energetic enemy.

He dismisses and damns, but despite himself, he hears."

*DRIVING PAST A BROKEN DOWN PICKUP FULL OF*
*MIGRANTS LATE FOR WORK IN WILLARD*


Hurry, good mechanic!
        Jiggle our hope and bleed the cables,
      blow on the fanbelt and jump our forgiveness.

These men are needed for cantaloupe,
      these women for harvesting peas.

Who will shuck and pod if not these chosen souls?
      Who will believe our dreams?
      Whose mothers will lay down in dust and wake in paradise?

O, make haste toward Jerusalem, my wandering children.
      Make haste and hay.

For behold, we will bear your iniquities,
      your rolling r's and suspect documentation —
      Your diligence will deliver you,

or if not you then your children. Or theirs.

Yea, I have seen the meek rise
        from cap to collar, from stiff to stamp,
      but each hour is a window closing,
      and the strawberries are impatient.

So hurry, grease your valves,
      seek solace in your neighbor's hunger.

For lo, the festival season approacheth like a highway patrolman,
      and no one can say what sacrifices will be required.

*DUE TO LIGHTED ARCHES ON HIGH STREET, COLUMBUS WAS,*
*FOR A TIME, KNOWN AS THE MOST BRILLIANTLY LIT CITY*
*IN THE COUNTRY*


We crash into town
via the brewery,
and eventually
find a snazzy bar
full of young lawyers
cutting their canines
at the state level
before opening
private practices.

On CNN is
a report about
the latest killings.
But what upsets J
is how they tune out.
One guy even says,
"Is there a game on?"
A bouncer has been
watching us not drink,
and before J says
more than, "Woe unto
you who eat old cheese
while the pillars sway —"
we're out on the street.

The looks they give us
as we're shuffled through
are honestly shocked.

How could anyone
get upset about
how they spend their nights?
Don't they work hard?
Aren't they helping
to protect the law
and the Buckeye State
from insurance fraud
and tax evasion?
And from real bad guys
who rape, kill, and steal?
Why shouldn't they want
a few hours some nights
to knock back a few
beers and think about
something that isn't
all that important?
It's not like they can
do a thing about
what is happening
over there, so what
is the big problem?
I don't disagree.
On the other hand,
if these "fine young men,
our warriors, our
grand stallions," don't care —
well, it's obvious.
For J, not caring
is the beginning
of the big meltdown.
Outside he's upset,
but I just drive us

to an empty lot,
unroll sleeping bags,
and count our money,
what's left of it.

Behold as I walk blistered down this rancid stretch of highway.

Who will believe me in my fury and costume?
　　　Even fencepost blackbirds
　　　　　turn dismissive shoulders away, barking.
And a lone neon billboard reads ADULT in simple satisfaction.

Am I mad or lost? Have I split open?
　　　For lo, words blast from my mouth before I think them,
　　　and halftimes I scarce believe them myself.

But look at this expanse of corn,
　　　at the brawny tractors loafing in the yards.
Are they not omens to be read? Do they not have
　　their significances?

And my bleeding feet? My cracked ear? My burned lip?
Do they not refer to the lame, deaf, and dumb
　　　who have been crushed by slogans
　　　　　since this road began to traverse the river?

By the waters of Muskingum I have wept and spat,
　　　pissed and dreamed.
My home is built on faulty foundations — it will collapse
　　in an instant.

I must hurry to speak before the paneling becomes my bones
　　　and the wallpaper my skin.

Hear, my people!
Abandon your fantasy leagues and your bogus committees!
The end of our championship run draws nigh,
    and no smiling governor can veto the decree.

*OHIO PORTRAIT IN 5-SYLLABLE ROAD SIGNS*

Woodchipper for Rent
Danger! Rocks Below!
Registered Holsteins
Adopt a Highway
Pres. Harding's Birthplace
Progressive Euchre
Troubled? Try Praying.
Soccer Conference Champs
Long Live Rock & Roll
Ceramic Lawn Pets
New Development
Re-elect John Glenn
The County's Best Yarn
Slippery When Wet
Sarah We Miss You
Hardy Mums for Sale
Private Property
Forget the Damned Dog —
        Beware of Owner!
Electric Co-Op
Next Stop Defiance
Wal-Mart Coming Soon

*RIGHT LANE MUST EXIT*


In Canton I bought a carton of Camels
      to show I was prepared to die. Here, orange

      smoke over the flavor factory reminds me
of safer houses. Pigeon scat streaks the overpass
      as these words stain my chin.

        Where have you been, o my comforter?
Who knows me better
      than you in your wet wool sweater?

For a while I fancied myself a paper crane —
      I was intricate and prone to luck. Now even
my arches are fallen. What I have seen

        in my once-proud towns
      could turn a brick brittle. Look —

the Ohio hills have gone blue like a cold lip.
      The boys I loved
have collapsed themselves in shame. They see now
        how they profited from prophets. Yea,

I could tell tall tales about our fancy wagons and smacked chins.
      I could belly up and bend dimes for spite.
                    But no —

I'll keep to this frantic caravan.
      So long as my alternator holds,
        I will blitz borders with the best.

Workmanlike, I shift and scan.

*ELEGY FOR THE TRUCK*


We were just
       hitting the outskirts of Ashland —
       the dead smokestacks, the cheerful billboards —

when the truck
       coughed, clanged, and started weaving right.
       I eased her to the highway's shoulder

and started
       cursing the day I was born, but
       Jeremiah stopped me with a laugh.

He climbed out
       and stroked the hood, head bent, as if
       he were listening for a voice from

the fan belt.
       A minute later he hefted
       his duffel bag and started walking.

I asked him
       if he had any damned idea
       how far we would be going tonight.

He answered,
       "We were without transportation
       at the beginnings of our journeys,

and we must
        always be prepared to hoof it.
        This steed has carried us far enough."

I was still
        thinking about the dispatcher
        in Circleville who'd want fourteen grand

once I was
        back home after all this madness.
        Then it struck me that I might never,

that I might
        just keep going. How long could I
        follow this man? How much would I change?

Before we
        lumbered down the next exit ramp
        I took a last look back at the truck.

How long would
        it take for the local bandits
        to strip it down to bolts and trinkets?

And is that
        some kind of weird resurrection?
        What would Jeremiah say to that?

There he was just walking down the street, singing.
Good day. Sunshine. Then he goes raising the roof.

Crashes into me wearing that same old shaggy dress.
I'm thinking, What's it all about?

He wants to hold my hand. He's funny that way.
I'm like, You'd better watch your step. You'll be a woman soon.

He shouts. Lets it all out. I know now.
It's your destiny to be the king of pain. So? Here we are.

Now entertain us. He started talking at me, Get up! Stand up!
It don't mean nothing. Not this time.

If you want to sing out, I'm your man. Roam if you want to.
But nothing's gonna change my world.

He can't hold back. Falls into a burning ring of fire,
calling out around the world.

Something in my heart keeps telling me, don't talk back.
But enough is enough. Can't stand no more.

I hit him with my best shot. Whoomp, there it is.
His eyes too bloody to see.

I could have danced all night, but Jane says,
Don't be cruel. Take me to the river.

*AFTERMATH*


I went out and bought a bag of carrots,
something good he could eat without his hands,
which were swollen, raw, and shiny with lymph.
I popped them in his mouth two at a time
while we worked our way back to the highway.

I said, "Listen, there are some people that,
no matter how you say it, no matter
how brave and beautiful your imagery,
they will never believe in you. Ever.
They will never turn." "If you believe that,"
he said, turning, stopping dead in his tracks,
and holding out his puffy hands like two
oven mitts to protect him from my heat —
"If you think that then you are a traitor
and a scoundrel, a damned carpet-bagger
and a mountebank. What are you here for
if not to change the hearts of the people —
all the people, every one. Some with words,
some with images, some by force of will,
some because of what they hear from others,
others because of what they think they hear.
Everyone must change or no one will be saved."

I woke from my dream of Lodi
and started on my journey.

It was just after sunrise. Small birds with big voices were
screeching in the little splotch of trees where we were sleeping next
to the highway. He sat up with a cough and began combing his
fingers through his beard, looking for ticks. I stoked coals to boil
our two eggs in the can of beans we ate last night. All gifts of a legal
secretary he terrified at lunch hour with words of warning:

Behold I set before you the ways of life and death —
Only by falling away can you live.

He chewed the egg without peeling it, then drank the water out of
the can, not even wincing at the hot metal on his mouth, though a
welt grew on his bottom lip that I had to salt to keep from bursting.

Bruce, you are a pillar in a garden of cucumbers.

Thanks. He must still be half asleep. I gathered my pack and a
couple of walking sticks, and we hopped the fence back to the
shoulder. Where to today, Quien no sabe?

To the city of iniquity, where parking meters
brutalize the passersby,
and street signs enforce the day. One way! One way!

What are you saying, I asked him. We haven't seen a one-way street
since we fled Columbus. Where to now, Cleveland?

It shall be a dwelling place for jackals,
an astonishment and a hissing.
The people will moan like pipes.

Sounds like Cleveland to me.

*SLOPPING IN THE RAIN BETWEEN WADSWORTH AND POE*


Yea, in the city I will speak the truth!
    Hey ho, the truth in the place of iniquity!

I will warn the people in their linen hearts,
    I will tell them to turn, turn, turn.

What more can I do but harangue when the sky
        hangs precarious
    like a vase on a lawn mower.

How can they fail to hear me,
        when they know
    I speak straight from the Source?

Their cellphones are magnets pulling,
    pulling them to another blank signal.

The people are lost without their wonder.
        They fuss and fret
    but have no fury.

Yea, I was sitting amidst the wrenches and petunias
    when the voice of the Lord
        came ringing down

like a gameshow winner's fanfare. It said,

Who will seize my country with conviction?
    Who will lead us into a new season?

Yo! I said. I'm your man. Send me.

But you are tarnished and despoiled,
            sad fool.
        You could not even care for a boy.
How can you save the whole people?

I don't know. I don't know. I don't know.

## AKRON'S HISTORY IS COLORFUL, PAINFUL, DIVERSE, AND INSPIRING

Some mornings he would wake me
        by declaiming while he pissed,
but others, I'd blink awake
        to find he'd cleared the campsite
and washed my clothes, hanging them
        on convenient pine branches.
He'd wait till I was fully
        alert, then he'd say, "Come now,"
and we'd be at it again.

Before, I'd thought about how
        this trip was helping me find
a tolerable version
        of the self I thought I'd lost.
But it was only after
        that awful night in Ashland —
nursing him, calming him down —
        that I started to believe
that I was meant to be here.

A little sympathy,
        a little frustration and luck
and all of a sudden
        you find yourself at the center
of something that becomes
        who you are for a while. Not quite
an accident. More like
        a mistake you were prepared for.

## BULLFROG JEREMIAH

In a distant lake before my boy was born
    I sank to my hips in mud
    and croaked an old song to the new reeds.

Where were my thrilled companions?
Behold they were scattered like beans in a pot,
    carapaces cracking.

You couldn't lob a grenade without hitting one,
    and so I did, rejoicing.

Yea, their cries of glory reached the heavens,
    but hardly broke the surface of the water
        where spray and stone intermingled.

Lord forgive me,
    I thought I had learned about grief in those waters,
        but I sit corrected.

Now I wait in Columbiana sludge with a bone in my back
    and Bruce gone to town for cabbage.

What ho, mosquitoes! Wherefore your biblical anger
   and insistence?
How can I absolve you when my blood has been drained
    like a spidered fly?

Why not follow me east and feast on the entrails of the cityfolk
instead of on an old man whose will is so blunt
    he can't chew through stew?

## JEREMIAH'S WOUNDS

First the heart, clogged crushed and clattered like a bus stop can of pop.

Then the creaky joints, as if he had been drained of fluids.

Various unmentionable digestive complaints.

Blackberry bush scratches on calves, cheeks, and forearms.

Broken tooth from cut-rate barber in Dry Fork.

Scraped up hands from misfired roundhouse in Pink.

Athlete's foot between fourth and fifth toes.

Sprained knee: wrong-end off-ramp tumble.

Cavity right bicuspid.

Bleeding ear from thrown stone.

Old wrenched wrestling hip.

Tree root stiff neck.

Blistered lip.

Fallen arch.

Hayfever.

Sunburn.

Shingles.

Piles.

Corns.

## JEREMIAH AT THE ALL SAINTS CATHEDRAL, YOUNGSTOWN


I embrace your iconography with its gold paint
                 and its tragic majesty.

I genuflect before the symbols of super-human suffering,
        while I suffer as a human,
                the only way I know how.

Surely you must see that your families
        are breaking apart like spring ice.

The heat comes from the east —
        we must douse it with our good deeds,

or it will crisp us like over-grilled cheese.

We must cleanse the city of its corruption manacles,
        its sadness and its fastfood chains.
We must let loose the Hun, and the drum, and the One.

        Behold I must speak with the king!
I must speak to the man who speaks like a king,
        and the man who speaks like a chipmunk.

I must convince them all to purge, to turn,
        to don this shirt of fine hair
and bore me with their righteousness.

Only then will I have performed my service.
        Only then will my boy rest.

Have we not earned our mistreatment?
Have we not shimmied and chastised and bowled?
Have there not been city council meetings and testimony
        that all should have attended
    but instead we were found lolling in lounge chairs
        or shopping for socks?

Engage, o my people! Be onerous and phrenetic!
    Be vicious with your systems!

Who knows but that your world will shake
        with the slip of an axle,
and your well-rehearsed unfeeling gloom
        suddenly burst claws of fire?

Will you tally yourselves among those
        who cared for rebel lieutenants?
Will you take your place with those
        who stripped off their suits for a swim?

J bowls through thicket and yon cursing sturdy billboard
construction, hair knotted up with last year's fallen oak bark.
Comes down on college town sweating lustily in the post-exam
heat and greet. Tank top and cut-off summer school not half bad if
you don't have to wrack your head against Org. J flusters into the
Snazzy Café proclaiming: *Cut off the foreskins of your hearts!* Lounging
crowd is, like, Word. Nod wink and grin at hapless barkeep
thinking, Always on my watch. Then smart-mouth part-time
landscaper-artist sidles forward with a new song: play? J flickers,
feints, forks rook with nifty knightmoves. Landscaper doesn't get
the joke. J vaguely victorious until drops sight of crucial bishop to
proclaim a moratorium on bug zappers. Endgame. Landscaper
won't accept his assignation. Launches into various hoots and
proofs. Don't play dumb, bum. J knocks a coffee overboard while
waving a despondent arm. Latte on lapel of grad stud reading
Hobbes at next table. J gets ugly tossed. Skins an elbow and limps
to campus nursing. Stashes sack in all-night computer lab and
wanders halls in mad lament till good-natured Ralph Duck sends
him on his way. Back to the highway withya, hobo. J says, Word.

*WHAT I'VE GOT SO FAR, APPROACHING YOUNGSTOWN AND
SEPTEMBER*


Buses are beautiful but billboards an abomination.

Highways lead to the circle of truth.

Walking is like sleeping because it contains waves and rhythms.

In the Jeremiah mind, Ohio is the desert.

Five miles outside of Ashland on Mud Lake Jeremiah found a fish
floating belly-up to the sun and thought it was worshipping.
Perhaps a carp, but probably stock bass or rockfish. In the Jeremiah
mind all things are searching for a way to sing to the heavens, and
dying in the shallow water is no less a way than shouting at the
passers-by on Route 250. Later we walked into a pizza joint called
Brothers where locals sourly dripped sauce onto their *Plain Dealer*
and he said,

> *Woe is the man who has lost his sense of taste.*
> *Woe is the woman who eats and finds no comfort.*

Being run out of town is not the same thing as being ignored.

In Jeremiah's mind the savage will win out on the street, but at
    night in their beds the people will begin to listen.

Once he said that eating gravel is an ancient form of holy speech.

In Jeremiah's mind we strayed from the path when we stopped
    stopping each other on the way to the grocery.

The silence as much as the hurry, the air conditioning and power windows, the drive-thru and the cellphone.

In his mind teenagers with headphones are an exception because even in their silence they speak to each other of their fear and loneliness.

To Jeremiah, there are those given righteousness, and those given other gifts, like football.

Nowhere, in anything he's said, is there a hint that what he has done, and what he is doing, and what he might do, is not part of a plan to bring the people back to each other. His trust is perfect, though he knows he will likely not witness the day. He is on point and will see action, but only the rear-guard will finish the victory.

Is that me?

In the Jeremiah mind the fields of Upper Sandusky are as desperate as the flophouses of Brooklyn, and he is on his way to the city to seek clues and offer comfort and admonishment.

In the Jeremiah mind the people will shout with him in the end.

## HITCHING A RIDE OUT OF CALIFORNIA, PA

If not for the moon which grows fainter each night,
    the Taco Bell would be the only light for miles.

Who will stop for me, here on this terrible gravel?
    Who will be my comfort and my keep?

I have counted six vans with their familiar passengers
    blasting exhaust on their way toward more fluorescent light.

They are all destined for dinner,
    and I for a mouthful of soot.

Who will take me if I raise my shoulder to the road?

Who will remember the promises on the sign outside of town:
    Welcome to California.

Well, come. For this battered brain basket, California has been
    a wretched bench, a lonely layover, a wash.

Even the secretaries smoking menthols outside the Third Fifth Bank
    dismissed my heartbreak.

They know more about the end of the world
    than the ends of their evenings.

Who will take me from this place
    and speak casually in the dashboard corona?
Who will let me climb into her flatbed?

I have washed my knees of the blood I lost from falling in the river, but am still stranded and far from my destination.

*SWEDISH IMMIGRANT CARL ERIC WICKMAN BEGAN*
*TRANSPORTING MINERS FROM HIBBING TO ALICE, MN, IN 1914*


Credit is a beautiful thing.
      Uncle Visa paid our way
            from State College

to New York. I was already
      in debt, so who cared about
            three hundred more?

I was feeling a bit giddy,
      and after I threw our bags
            onto the bus

I treated us to a gorgeous
      dinner at Ponderosa —
            steak, potato,

crazed bounty of the salad bar.
      They even served us little
            bowls of ice cream.

Jeremiah assumed that I
      was trying to fortify
            us for the trip,

and for whatever would come next.
      He wasn't far off, although
            there was a bit

of the relief of the condemned
in my self-destructive splurge.
In any case

Jeremiah expressed his thanks
by telling me about Ben,
his son who died.

Since Pittsburgh I had been trying
to think of a way to ask
about his son —

I'd try to refer to the time
before he started preaching,
but he'd always

turn it back to something about
the way Mt. Orab was sure
to disappear

now that the people had traded
their goodly inheritance
for chocolate sauce.

He described the boy in a voice
I had never heard before —
almost toneless.

In truth he sounded like any
good Midwestern kid to me —
clean, plain, decent,

never without a baseball cap,
    drank beer sometimes, loved his car.
        A bit boring.

But the way J spoke about him —
    well, I guess it's how all men
        talk about sons,

except that no men talk like him.
    Still, for that meal he was just
        a normal man

trying to understand a loss
    that was simply beyond his
        capacity.

He called him, "My olive orchard,"
    and as I ushered him back
        to the station

I promised myself I wouldn't
    abandon him, at least till
        I could be sure

he had someone else to care for.
    I didn't keep that promise,
        not remotely.

*PONDEROSA CONFESSION*

There were fields, and there were folds in the fields.
There were geometric adventures and theoretical flowers.

The boy was born broken from the womb
of our Chevrolet. Said, Don't tell Dad,

then slipped. Into.
The folds of his coat, far off in the flax,

hid a flask half full of coffee. I nearly laughed
to taste it, still warm in the morning.

I have seen my fill of suffering — slash-backed terriers
and broken-cheeked wives, men watching their own deaths

approach up a creaky escalator. I have watched a cat-
ravaged field mouse convulsing in confusion: why can't I run?

But why should I be born to labor and sorrow
in this land of rusted barnyards and collapsed school buses

if all my hopes would skid across the asphalt to bury themselves
in rows not yet in bloom? Yea, the jackals

cackle on my stoop. You have not seen the worst,
they tell me. If this is so,

then how can I be silent?
How can I not shout the only way I know how?

## VILLANELLE FOR JEREMIAH'S SON

My only son had a scar on his cheek
in the shape of a Nike swoosh.
I am wretched. I will not be consoled.

He earned it on his Norco mountain bike
in a state which has no mountains.
It was Ohio slate that marked his cheek.

From the glowing porch I watched him flip
over the handlebars onto his face.
He was furious. He would not be consoled.

His death, too, was crammed with brands.
Logos on his T-shirt, hat, Camaro —
peeled bottles in the trunk lying cheek to cheek.

Even the hospital had its sympathetic logo
that gazed warmly in the lobby's light.
I paced awry. I would not be consoled.

Their words were shorthand for failure.
It was the "nothing we could do."
I identified him by the scar on his cheek.

I gave his eyes to Iowa, his kidney
to an angry diabetic from Duluth.
She didn't want it. She would not be consoled.

At the home, I stayed until they all were gone.
The boys wore their father's suits,
and I kissed them on their oily vibrant cheeks.

I have lost my olive harvest.
I have lost my magic touch.
My only son had a scar on his cheek.
I am empty. I will not be consoled.

*JEREMIAH, PA*


Hear me while I call out my affliction
        up in the smelly belly of this Greyhound Express.


                I am hunched over a lunch
of cold chicken fingers,
and the eight hours to the city are laid out before me
like a long day's work cutting stone.
                                Hear me,
you varsity girls kneeling on your seats:
your hiphop slang won't save you from the army jackets
and oily slacks in back!
                        Listen you driver, strung out
from last night's haul from Moab! And you, old woman,
with phantasmal hair beneath your shawl.


        Hear the voice of an old caterer
who has buried his share of sons.


The hills are tired of wearing mud
the color of an old sock.
                        Yea, the wind
whistles warnings through the cracked windshield,


and we are pilgrims through a ravaged land.
Our eyes will find no comfort here.
                                Buried are the bones
of those who broke the first trails
from the Alleghenies, and forgotten their sons
who built shelters of pine bark. Indeed we must be

the last of the righteous.
It is for our sake the world still spins.

    Therefore must we rake
our fingers across the vinyl seats, my friends,
and readjust the rearview mirrors.
                              Let us align
the tires and cancel our plans for the afternoon.

      For though our eyes burn
with grimy soot from the road,
we shall be renewed as in the days of old.
Listen to the diesel engine coughing a tune for our new song.

## PAY WHEN BOARDING

The bus took us as far as Wilkes-Barre
before they tossed us off for being too
disruptive. As if riding a Greyhound
from State College to New York requires some
contemplation, quiet, and solitude,
despite the gaseous groan of the engine
and the sad loneliness of everyone
on board — grandmothers on a last visit
to their sisters' homes, hungover students,
and rank vagabonds chasing one last ace.
Maybe it was the weather, but we all,
even Jeremiah, felt bleak and wet.

Somewhere around Lewisburg I climbed back
and took a tired piss, weaving with the road
and the sickly blue-green slosh in the bowl.
It occurred to me, as I stared down there,
that this man needs more help than I can give,
and that much more may be too much for me.
J seemed agitated, imagining
what would happen to him in the city.
His knee bobbed and he gnawed his cuticles.
When had he last been to New York City?
Had he ever? In a place filled throat-high
with prophets, seers, and half-baked crazy-men,
could anyone differentiate J
from the usual street quacks and wackos?
Could the people recognize his wisdom?
Now, when it wouldn't be in some nameless
two-bit decimated Midwestern town

but in the center of the universe,
where the world happened, where
people you didn't know could kill, arrest,
or anoint you.
                    And I wasn't ready.
The truth is I goaded him into his
Greyhound harangue. First I asked him about
the mining towns here in Pennsylvania,
about the stripped woodlands and poisoned streams,
the cowed company towns and strike-breakers.
At first he answered me like a tired prof —
"Well, you see, my boy . . ." But as soon as I
pointed out a sign for an old dry goods
store that had been renovated into
a Chili's, something clicked. I knew it would.
He stood in his seat, back to the window,
to survey the riders with their blank stares,
calloused and suspicious.
                              I just wanted
a few more days with the Jeremiah
I believed, before we made it to town
and I cut myself loose.

*PSALM OF SCRANTON*

And a woman there served me eggs.
Over hard. Oil

crackling on the decimated white. No
shoes no shirt and yet
                              she served me. Yea,

Grace still struggles on this earth,
          in her gray apron.
                              Woman of vigor!
Woman of lonely hills! Cracked
cuticles and a slipped disk will not be the sum
                    of your inheritance! Even now,

lined along the noose of highways that surround this city,
            mile markers are counting out our longings,
        tallying our deeds and misdeeds,

and for the righteous there will be a long rest in Bermuda,
a new couch, another son. I declare it
                              who am the voice of justice.
I have scoured out my house with chalk.
                              Dear woman,
          remove your hair net and your tarnished trinkets.
Slough off your loss and chewing gum.

          Tomorrow I turn my feet to that great
city by the waters, but tonight I may yet bathe and sleep.

*JEREMIAH DEFACES A ROADSIDE SHRINE*

J buttonholes a bored local at a truckstop trading post where air-freshening cardboard cutouts hang from hooks next to other ineffective icons, and crabby clerks distribute telephone change to wind-fried drivers in oil-stained overalls. Calls himself Alter. He's chewing a jerk. What ho! calls J. Before I met you I knew your uncle. Alter says he's built a shrine of apple cores beside the creek, and J may worship there if he wears trousers. So. J hefts his sack and follows past the guard rail and sound barriers, over a swarm of revolutionary gravestones, and past flax fields drained of ambition. Alter hikes with a hitch in one hip, and at a stone wall he's so winded he can only point with his stick to a splotch of trees between the knees of two opposing hills. J leaves him wheezing. Down the slope a blackbird launches invectives. There, under a sprawling pine, along with a broken cup and assorted needles, is the Sanctuary, a pyramid of browned, flea-frittered Golden Delicious, piled high as a hip. O You and Your fancy handiwork, Old Decorator. J cracks a can and pours soup around the space as libation. Chipmunks chatter in the branches, and J declares a day for decay and concentration. Alter, your shrine is the holiest construction site in Pennsylvania. May your children grow large in the contemplation of its mystery and promise.

*JEREMIAH AT BEIS T'FILLAH OF TEANECK*

Here is the house where the men and women
    divide themselves

so that the women may be more brave, and the men
    more generous.

Hello, good my people! Have you seen the bridge
    to desolation?

Have you clutched your skull with its inner noise
    and broken

your registers, reaching for the light? Or have you
    slandered in suits,

and studied Mishnah while your sons coughed and worried?

Woe unto thee, o my auditors! Woe upon your contracts
    and calculators!

Learn your texts and sing them! Do and then hear,
    o my menschen!

Arise now, arise and march with me
    to the island of iniquity.

We'll each take a corner and shout out to the streetlights.

We'll split the pavement with our eloquence and tribulations.

Who can resist us? Who can deflect our fear and fire?

Behold we will bury the venial in verbiage. They will must
     be moved.

And when all the corners are covered and converted,
     then may we disperse

back to our happy hamlets and developments —
     we'll dismantle our gates

and dismember our security systems. We'll smash
     our modems with vigor and exaltation.

We will be fresh from our convention. We will
     preach and prove.

Yea, march with me, my ancient brothers! Show me
     you know what I mean!

Be not doctors and brokers and salesmen. Be priests.
     Be Nazarenes.

*JEREMIAH'S BLUES ON THE GW BRIDGE*

This end of the Sound is a river, this end of my mind one hair,
This end of the Sound is a river, this end of my mind one hair,
My torn tongue's tired of teaching, and I'm only halfway there.

O decrepit borough, splayed out like a skinned skunk,
O decrepit borough, splayed and rank like a skinned skunk,
This leg of your great city is lined with grime and junk.

My people breathe exhaustion, they don't fight it anymore,
Lord, my people breathe exhaustion, they don't fight it anymore,
Clouds ripe from their desires, smoke from forgotten doors.

I've got no email EZPass to speed me safe to Queens,
I've got no email EZPass to speed me safe to Queens,
I've just got words and rhythm, and the prophecies I've seen.

I've seen the passing tankers, with their loads of oil and grease,
I've seen the passing tankers, with their loads of oil and grease,
They push upriver pendulous, then descend into dis-ease.

Hey you toll booth operators, stranded like broken-soled shoes,
Hey you toll booth operators, stranded at your posts like shoes,
Go home to your plaid couches, let the diesel trucks blast through.

Let them carry their convictions upstate where they belong,
Let them carry their convictions upstate where they belong,
All they've left behind are napkins, and invoices they tallied wrong.

Here come some good policemen to pull me off the ledge,
Here come some well-trained, hard-worked, chapped lip,
         honest poor policemen, here to pull me off the ledge,
What they'll get for their good intentions is an earful of my rage.

MANHATTANVILLE EXPANSION RAISES QUESTIONS
ABOUT AESTHETICS


I'd forgotten Manhattan has hills,
and willfully ignorant oak trees.
South of the bridge, we climbed up a pile
of boulders, leaf mulch, and plastic bags,
and ate tuna sandwiches, looking
across the river at Cliffside Park
while commuters crammed and made gestures.
J was quietly popping his jaw.
His breath smelled like fish and sweet mint gum,
and I was silently thinking through
what my options were for escape.
"Are you ready?" I asked him, half-desperate.
*No. I don't know what will happen here.*
*The people . . . may not listen to me.*
"They must," I said, wanting to believe.
"Besides, don't all prophets have that fear?"
*For good reason. The people don't have*
*a great batting average when it comes*
*to heeding God's word.* "I don't either."
Then he stood. *To whom shall you pay heed?*
*To whom swear allegiance? Your cable?*
*A cash-mad pop-gun corporation?*
*To bogus anger or blasé faiths?*
*I am He! I have something to say!*
A jogger turned but didn't break his stride.
J laid his hand on my sore shoulder
and sat down to finish his tuna.

*CHURCH OF THE INTERCESSION*


Begin you braying trumpets. Begin you fruitful stares.
I bring you my heartburn,
      my rancor and verve.

I lay them at your altar alongside the candlewax
      and hunger.

Yea yo, you cowards and corporate aspirants!
      You flagrant fouls and fugitive fortune tellers!

Where is your bubble?
      Your hi-dee-ho and 401k?
It has purchased some infant's afghan.

And you, who once raced the alleys in terror and surprise:
      where is your alibi? Your stink? Your crying uncle?

O, even the archway over 125th Street calls down for absolution.

The M5 fumbles down and down, carrying its load
      of househelp and entrepreneurs,
            its waifs and wannabes.

But where is the city and its electric tale?
      Where is your will to remake and remodel?

Yea, you have capsized the island, mi amigos.
      Your ceremonials and serial monogamies
         signify nothing before the Lord.

It is not enough to strive, o my people.
    We must reconfigure the equipment.
    You must see the drain and piping
before this year has shelved your dreams like swimwear.

*HANANIAH*

Word from Boob the Pen Man was he'd come from out West, some
first round draft pick prophet with corn fluff in his hair, and a
method actor on his tail taking notes and paying fines. He had a
rhythm, though, give him that. Knew how to sing a tune. But this is
my corner, only I harangue with the drang and bang that brings in
the cling, if you know what I mean. He was trying his luck with the
hot dog junkies and flyboys and was off-putting my beat with the
cheats and the freaks, so I parlayed over for a shuffle-on, hand on
blade. No need, though. He headed south like a good white man
should. Fucker must really think he's got the word. I feel for the
guy. I feel like smacking him upside the head. Should know by now
that prophecy is an art with no audience, just practicers.

*REDEMPTION OF THE FIELD AT BROADWAY AND 88TH*


Cousin, this is my ancestral square.

My hapless forefathers tilled it
  from the time of the good judges.

You have been a worthy caretaker,
  indeed a fine custodian
protecting the soil with this slab of cement
  and dressing it with your coat and bags —

yea, you have erected a shelter on this land,
  a sukkah of cardboard grapefruit cartons.

But though you have tended it well,
  I have returned from my sojourn in the West
    and I will redeem this plot again for my use.
Do not protest and risk the wrath of this bandage.
  Fear not for a fair price. I've got a slew of nickels.

I will claim my right of inheritance,
  my square of concrete, my little kingdom.
    And I will build a house to house my house.
  See, I have seed and a child's spork
to till the dormant ground.

There will be zucchini on the roadway.
  This field will bloom again.

## GENTRIFICATION OF UPPER MANHATTAN IS NOT YET COMPLETE

Jeremiah loved the sidewalks
    with their chewing gum beauty marks
        and their proud manufacturer's stamps.
    He'd stoop to trace the wild patterns

as if reading tea leaves. People
    would always look at him when he'd
        stop to make a declaration.
    It was only the New York *What?!,*

but was refreshingly direct
    after our weeks of Midwestern
        sideways avoidance. They didn't
    find him strange, or they didn't find

his strangeness strange. They stepped aside
    and went their way, some listening.
        Is there hope in this, old prophet?
    When I betray you, will those looks

sustain you in your confinement,
    while they decide where you belong?
        God, I'm tired. How can I do this?
    What else am I supposed to do?

## AT THE CONVERTED BANK

In the morning I heard the voice
        outside the dear old drug bank,
the mortgaged mortgager on Broadway and 76th.

Go, it said, go to the newsstand and eat the worst words,
        the false claims and natty explanations.

Then procure a shopping cart from the lonely men
        in their haze of concrete dust,

fill it with good eggs and lay down inside
        so the yolk flows in your hair.

Thus will I break the brains of the burgs and burbs,
        for they have soiled my streets

with their wrangling and whine. I will feed them
        wormwood and Saran.

They will taste the fruits of their labors.

What do I care for pennants and anthems,
        when cabbies strangle for cable?

Where are my altars and arks?
What's become of this house that once helped
        Pashtuns open groceries

and fronted greasy spoons? My loan and trust
        has collapsed into a pill panderer.

Pills for potency! Pills for prayer!
Do they not see
        that like the sea they can

toss themselves against the sand, but they cannot prevail?
Though they roar like waves, they will not pass.

Soon Nebuchadnezzar will make his public appearances.
I bequeath it all to him.
        All the wires and wireless,

all the blunt banners and butchers.

*OUR PEOPLE. OUR WORK. OUR VALUES.*


I am speaking into one of the last
      living payphones in Manhattan.
          The mouthpiece feels

as if it had been rubbed with Vaseline
      and I can smell someone else's
          breath in my voice.

I am telling the 911 lady
      that my old friend has lost his mind
          and I'm worried

that he may hurt himself or someone else.
      *He's yelling at the cough syrup.*
          And the woman

assures me that someone is on their way.
      Already I can hear sirens.
          All over soon.

J is escorted from the premises
      by a Latino rent-a-cop
          and instantly

sees me across the street, speaking
      with my hand covering my face.
          He grasps the arm

of the guard, and just then a huge airplane
    shrieks overhead, heading east to
        La Guardia.

I can almost hear the synapses snap.
    Before I can hang up the phone
        he jaywalks south

across 66th Street and starts sprinting.

Eicha!
The wall is breached, o my people!
    The supports and ramparts languish together!
We have been struck with steel streamers,
    and the shattered sky trembles!

    Behold, I will not spare the tall,
the twin, the terrific, the tasty or triumphant.
    They will all collapse like cans in a crusher.
The king has been called and is preparing his household for the worst.

Yea, they come from the North and we cannot repel them.
    They come from the East and we cannot flee.
They come from the West and we cannot resist them.
    They come from the South for our pretty ones.

See how we weep for our children,
    and refuse to be comforted.

By the time I could catch up with him
we were across the street from Lincoln Center.

There was a bright billboard announcing
Branford Marsalis was playing that evening.

I came up from behind and just walked
alongside a bit so he wouldn't startle.

He didn't recognize me at first.
He was fully in the swirl of it. But then

he whipped around like he'd heard a shot.
He seized my arms and said, *Now. Are* you *ready?*

His eyes were fierce and blazing with tears.
I don't think I am. He said, *Too late!,* and turned,

calling, First save the secretaries!
Then the janitors and early morning hacks!

His tone had changed. He wasn't angry.
He was hysterical, moaning and waving

his hands as if his mouth were burning.
And the list of grievances had turned to griefs.

That's when it finally dawned on me.
He thought the planes had just hit the Towers,

and he was heading to Ground Zero
to offer admonishment to the people.

I half-suspected that he was thrilled,
that 9/11 was what he'd predicted,

that he wanted to get to the site
to gloat, to revel in the horror of it.

I was completely wrong about that,
and should have known better. I should have known

that he was reliving another
bright clear morning and that everything had fused.

It was all the same pain to him now —
the firefighters, his son, the city, his son.

*ACROSTIC LAMENT*

Ah, she is awry! And all her beauty is anguish!
 Behold the broken bone of my bold city,
City that once clamored and careened like a caffeinated Doberman.
 Dust is now her dessert, death her deal.
Even the elms embrace ash and filthy embers;
 Forgotten are her favorites, aflame her great fortress.
Gone are the good, the governed, the greedy, and the gallant!
 Heavy-hearted, her heroines inquire, "How did this happen?" O!
I am ill with imagery, with the imagined, the imminent, and "this just in."
 Jarred, even rage escapes me. I am havocked.
Killers and kings alike are keeled over with shock. Yea, our loss is
 kaleidoscopic,
 Looming large like some magnificent Leviathan,
More mountain than monster, a new feature of our minds and memory.
 Never again will nerds, nymphs, or nurses need reminding.
O, my people! My oatmeal-eaters and olive pressers!
 Petty and pathetic seem the predictions I pandered from Quarry
  to Passaic.
Quaint and quirky my omens! How quickly my regular rants and
 Ridiculous ravings have assumed sinister resonances!

Still, I will say my piece amidst these stones. Stay sturdy, fellow citizens!
 Tomorrow the Twin Towers will again teach us transcendence.
Unfasten the umbrellas of your souls! Unleash your uncles' vitality!
 Verily will our valiant wills be revamped into vigor.
Wherever we wander we will wage war on excuses and weariness.
 Except for our expressions, we will nix our excesses and yearn
  for examples.
Young girls will yell in yellow jumpers. Yea, Your city will rise,
 Zestier than it was, wiser and more zaftig, zealous to be Zion!

## COME SPEND A GREAT DAY DOWNTOWN

But we were still something
        like eighty blocks from where
he thought we were going,

and I didn't believe
        he could maintain the pace.

Even by his standards
        he was revving too high.

Should I hail a taxi?
        The cops? An ambulance?

Then we hit Times Square
        and he fit right in.

A woman calling
        herself Naked Cow

was playing guitar
        in a star-spangled

bikini next to
        a mime decked out as
Lady Liberty.

There were young hawkers
        and young hawks and J,
                in his element,
spread his arms out wide.

It turns out even
the fiercest prophets
        change to comforters

once the disaster
        has befallen us.

And at the northeast
        corner of Broadway
                and 47th

he found the ruins
        he was looking for:

a construction site
        that was mostly hole

with a few broken
        bricks and 2 x 4s.

He slipped through the fence
        and rubbed gray fistfuls

of dust on his face
        while the hard hats gaped.

*DECLAIMING FROM THE WRECKAGE*

Be encouraged, you sons of Scarsdale!
    Let your faith sprout fringes!

Indeed a new hour clicks on the bank clock.
    Behold, the towers tremble

and tumble into reeking estuaries, and drywall dust
    pollinates the air.

From coast to coast our televisions groan
    with the weight of their messages.

But there is green in this pit. There is an artesian
    herb garden.

Let not this cataclysm be lost on us! Let us not
    find fault in our pockets.

We have been anointed with fire, with terror
    and error.

We are a chosen generation.
    Here is the sign we awaited.

Let us then compose a new tractate. Let us
    lend lawnmowers and Allegra

to our Armenian neighbors. Let the radio
    summon church mothers

from their candlecare and grant them dispensation.
  Let secretaries conduct

diplomacy from their cuticle cubicles.
  I have seen a vision of a world

suspended on a rock over the ocean, and believe
  in our precarious certainty.

Surely the day has come when we will all
  hold meetings underground

and make scratches with matches. Let mall food
  be served to our arachnid brethren.

See here in this wreckage the blueprints
  of a new city by the waters.

It didn't take long.
      Security guards
appeared by verse two
      and when they couldn't
chase him off the site
      they called the police
over from the street.

Like boxers the cops
      flanked and harried him
into a safe corner
      then calmly grabbed him.
They held his arms down,
      put him in their car
and swung the door shut.
      Simple E.D.P.

I watched everything
      from the safety of
the sidewalk, then backed
      myself to the curb.
I let them take him.
      I just let him go.

Look, it's not like we don't have other things to do. You'd think we're just standing around answering tourists' questions and nabbing pickpockets, but since 9/11 we've had extra training — you wouldn't believe the number of potential threats we hear about every week. Bebetista and me had our eyes peeled for a well-dressed Tunisian with a yellow backpack. Meanwhile this nutcase is yelling his head off inside the fence, trying to get himself hurt, grabbing people's collars and rubbing dirt on his face. Mostly the workmen just shoved him out of the way, and once I swear I saw him flat on his back, yelling away and covered in so much dust he looked like a goddamn ghost. But then he tried to grab a shovel, and the security guy got scared. So I said to Officer Kochmar, "Look, Terry, let's put him in a car until he cools down." We let him simmer until our shift was over. Can you believe the guy was still carrying on — didn't shut up the whole time, not when we drove him back, not when they hosed him down, not when one of the boys gave him a blap across the mouth and threw him in a cell with the rest of the night's take. He made it sound like it was 9/11 all over again and, to be honest, none of us were sure he wasn't telling the truth. It wasn't until one of the guys inside — some junkie we'd picked up around 2 a.m. — asked him straight up if he'd seen what had happened. Then he dropped it down to a normal level. I came in later, and he had them all sitting on the floor around him like a bunch of kindergarten kids. He was telling the story and describing everything like he'd been personally inside the planes, the building, everywhere all at once. The drunks were blubbering like babies. Then, here's the best part. He led them all in a chorus of "Yankee Doodle": *Yankee Doodle keep it up, Yankee Doodle dandy*. What do you say to that?

I was too tired to wander.
    Even standing on the curb —
with the billboard screens flashing,
    and the traffic, and the people —
was exhausting. So I did
    what any tourist would do:
I got rush tickets to see
    *Hairspray*, with Michael McKean.
Lord knows I know where I've been.

Up in the third balcony,
    surrounded by high schoolers
on a day trip from Greenwich,
    I recounted all my sins,
and repented with Edna.
    O, I bawled like a baby,
despite the teachers' shushing.
    What was happening to us?
Outside the whole world has crashed,
    and there I was, keeping time
with the unionized pit band.
    I am back in the vacuum.

If I hadn't picked him up,
    if I had just let him rave
until the local police
    brought him back to his people
would he be safe now? And me,
    would I still be hauling cakes?
Did I abet his madness?

Did I help make it, driving
him not like a chauffeur, but
        like a jockey? Or was that
just what was wanted from me?

After the show I walked south.
        It took less than two hours.

*FINGERPRINTING*


Fear not, young men of Judah!
      We will be hauled from this hole by the shoulders.
        Yea, we will be lifted like infants.

What sins you have committed before the Mayor,
      He will commute.
      Your fatal errors will not compute.

Here, take this ticket and stumble home
      like the rest of the fumblers and tumblers.

Friends, I have seen you in your oblivion.
      I know of your petty theft and possession,
and I have sent a shock to shake you.

Look around and tell me you see no message.

Behold I have marched from the marshes,
      and fled from fields to tell you this.

It is a big day, good sons. Yea, a whopper.
      Do not fail your ancestors who knew destruction
        like an annoying uncle at the table.
Nay, yield not to your usual sad-sack escapisms.

Be steadfast with your spirits!
      Do not neglect to floss!

The ink on your hand is a stain on your hearts.
      Cleanse not with the cleanser, but with your tongues!

We had been spared the scary until now.
Let us not flinch before the mighty needle delivers
its purging medicine.

*SONG OF REPENTANCE*

I have learned to think less of myself, because
   I haven't learned to think less of myself.

*SUPPORT THE INTERNATIONAL BROTHERHOOD OF*
*ELECTRICAL WORKERS*


The fence was so high around the site
   that from some angles it's just a glow
from the klieg lights and sounds from workmen
   clearing the debris and putting down
the foundations of the new Towers.
   All to be finished by 2012.

I pulled out some of my transcriptions
   that had rolled themselves into a scroll
at the bottom of my pack, and read.
   I read, in full voice, under a light
at Church and Dey. I read, not because
   I thought it was the Holy Temple,
and not because its destruction meant
   anything I can articulate,
but because J wanted to speak here
   and I was part of preventing it.
I read the whole sheaf, until sunrise,
   and then I found an all-night diner
and had a quiet pile of pancakes
   before heading back up to Times Square
to find the precinct where they held him.
   If nothing else, if absolutely
nothing else, I had to bring him home.

Words come to me out of the nowhere that
  the locals call the sky.

Here in this pit I gather them into piles,
  like toenail clippings.

You are wondering,
  What makes a man shout from streetcorners,
  break his lungs for the sake of glory,
    believing himself some sorry emissary?

My answer: when he hears the words
  and they are so full of melody, how can he
    not let them sing?

Of course there are the soldiers to cart me away,
  and the King does as his advisers advise.
This is as I have been warned
    by good people in diners and buses.

When I began my journey,
  I was in the thrall of a grief greater
than my mouth could encompass.

I have held the broken bone between my palms
  and done nothing.
I have caressed death with longing.

  Now I sit in this pit
with a hammer for a tongue and anvil teeth.

Lend me your hardest metal, and I will
    bend it into a pretzel.

Give me a tube of simple glass,
    and I will make it weep.

I am not finished with my prayers and preachings,

and will see another sunrise
    before the dust clears from this cell.

Take care of my father.
      Yea, be his proper prop.
Take him by the elbow
      And guide him home to me.

Take care of my prophet.
      Yea, be his faithful scribe.
Take down his every word
      And bring him home to me.

Take care of my people.
      Yea, be their clearest eye.
Take in their fear and grief
      And lead them home to me.

## ITEMS IN THE PRISONER'S POSSESSION

Assorted worthless artifacts removed from construction site:

papers, part of a seat cushion, the key to a file chest.

Photograph of prisoner with son, neither smiling.

Steel-toed boots, worn down to a pair of moccasins.

Sweatshirt: "Property of Cincinnati Reds."

Old sleeping bag smelling of cat urine.

Pack of Wrigley's Spearmint Gum, opened.

Two dollars twenty-seven cents.

Map of Ohio, tattered.

Three pairs soiled underwear.

Four greasy T-shirts.

Army duffel.

Can, baked beans.

Bible.

Belt.

*EMOTIONALLY DISTURBED PERSONS MAY BE RELEASED INTO*
*THE CUSTODY OF FAMILY MEMBERS AT THE DISCRETION OF*
*THE COMMANDING OFFICER*


When he came out
they had just given him back his things
              and he was holding them tight

        to his chest like
any refugee. I was so glad
              to see him I nearly broke his back

        hugging so hard.
But he was quiet, pale and subdued
              until we left the precinct.

        He looked at me
and smiled with a rusty tenderness,
              holding my arm down the stairs.

        Outside he said,
"Bruce, they are more like you than I thought."
              What do you mean? Like me how?

        "The people here —"
He waved his arm across Manhattan.
              "They fear souls like they fear rats.

        "Now they're waiting
to be told how to 'channel their grief.'"
              I asked, "But shouldn't they, now?

"Won't we be changed?"
"Yea, you will be. To snapping turtles.
            You will learn to eat your young."

    We walked a bit,
heading east, but before we had gone
            three blocks, J was out of breath

    and had to rest.
We found a park bench and J slumped down,
            suddenly a frail old man.

    I had worried
about his mental health since the day
            we met in Chillicothe.

    But I hadn't
ever thought about his strength until
            the hour we spent on that bench.

    Then he sprang up.
and started heading north, double-time.
            "Not finished yet!" he called back.

    The streets wheeled by,
and then there was Port Authority.

The first commuters were disembarking in their sad suits for another day's work. J surveyed the board like he was reading a menu, but there was only one place to go now.

Come, my prophet, let us sail from this destruction
       and worm our way back over the Alleghenies.

    *Yes, let us return to my rivers and fields.*

So then? Are you free? Has your tongue let go of you? Is your son at rest?

    *No, dear fool, we must spread the news!*
        *The villages must hear our depositions!*

    *O, Bruce, the harvest is past, the summer over,*
        *and still the people grieve.*

    *We are a long way from saved.*

    *But I know an old soldier in Mt. Gilead*
        *who might sell me some special lotion . . .*

I'll get him home and we'll go from there.

    *Fear not, fair wanderer.*
        *Neither be dismayed.*

    *Even the suckers will get their succor.*
        *Even the slaves will sleep.*

Two for Cincinnati, please.

*NEWARK LOCAL*


Lord, I am weary as an old mop.

I have nearly emptied my pockets
    and spent my last — no.

Enough! Begone, cowed canker!
    Away, weariness and grief!

There is already too much tragedy on the Turnpike today.
    I will withhold my contribution.

See how even the exit signs plead and pulse.

Yea, though my heart burns and my neck
    creaks and cracks,
    yet will I urge, cajole, bluster and muster.

For indeed we are a holy people.
Yea, see our hodgepodge and hullabaloo.

We have built more cities on hills
    than all the ants of the Amazon.

But we still do not know the path to righteousness,
    o my soul.

Those who say so are false teeth and toupees.

Behold we are lonely emperors.
We are coyotes in strip malls.
We are lost bees.

Send us your wisdom and discretion, o lord.
Renew us as in the days of old —

Not as they were, but as we imagined them.

*FORTY-TWO PERCENT OF GREYHOUND PASSENGERS ARE*
*BETWEEN THE AGES OF 18 AND 34*

Jeremiah's preachings on the bus
  weren't loud enough to cause
    any disturbance,

but just after we hit the Turnpike
  he started to shiver and
    vomit on his shirt.

The driver pulled into a rest stop
  and helped me carry him off,
    shouting, "Get help fast!"

Someone called 911 and someone
  else found a first-aid kit, but
    all it had inside

were gauze pads and old disinfectant.
  J wiped his chin with paper towels
    and sat on the curb.

"I'd like a bag of potato chips,"
  he said, and slumped into me.
    I could hear sirens

but everything was moving so damned
  slowly, and all I could do
    was put my hand down

to support his weight. "You'll go home now,
    Bruce Gray, and resume your search
        for the righteous path."

"I'll try to follow yours," I told him,
    my shaky voice informing
        me I was weeping.

"No, you'll go home and count syllables.
    And I will die in exile
        like a good prophet.

Remember me to the folks back home,
    but don't try to sell my house.
        That's for the termites."

The EMTs did their best with him,
    but we figured the attack
        had started before

we had even gotten on the bus.
    The first time he felt pain and
        didn't need to shout.

How I wanted to see a vision then
but nothing came. No religious rapture,
no love at first sight, no criminal scheme.
I escorted Jeremiah's body
back to Mt. Orab, where he was buried
alongside his beloved wife and son.
Local people came to pay their respects —
neighbors, congregants, former co-workers.
Some of Ben's classmates had kids of their own.
Afterward, someone had a barbecue
and we traded stories — early for late.
I spent the night on someone's pleather couch.

At dawn I hoisted my backpack and looked
at the hills, sleepy with fall's early mist.
I felt cold, wet, and raw, ready to walk.

How simple it is to die
　　　at the Walt Whitman rest area,
　　　　　in view of the swamp and trash,
　　　　　in the thrall of my people's hurry.

How they skip from their burgers to their seatbelts,
　　　offering coffee to their dashboards,
　　　cradling the cups as carefully
　　　　　as they'd hold their daughter's eye.

How simple it is to die,
　　　with nothing accomplished,
　　　the people in exile and our palace in ruins.

Our learned men have fled,
　　　our holy rollers are just getting going.

But I will not see the restoration.
　　　I will be long gone to swamp feed.

Bruce, you mustn't take me the wrong way.
　　　I am an eggshell, a used cocoon.
　　　I've seen enough to say I've seen enough.

Still, I would have liked to feel
　　　the hungry heat of another fire.

*SONG OF LEAVING*


Not wanting to lose them,
we travelers have tattooed hearts
into our arms and ankles.
            Starlings outside
forage through take-out containers,
and Hyundais hum like children chewing.
We are still here. Still
here, dropping dimes into
the unmarked box next to the register.
Still winking at the skinny cashier,
and the thin music seeping from invisible speakers
is our cloak and cover.
O, to have been led to shimmering vistas —
We want to be more than we're worth,
more than statements, warnings,
broadcasts, break-ups, and beer.
Here there's still love and debt —
The janitor breaks from mopping
to wring his wrists
while spilled liquid trickles and pools, trickles and pools.
Hover over my shoulder, shadow.
Bless my lands and people.

AUTHOR PHOTO © BARBARA STONEHAM

## ABOUT THE AUTHOR

*ADAM SOL* is the author of two previous collections of poetry, *Jonah's Promise*, which won the Mid-List Press's First Series Award for Poetry, and *Crowd of Sounds*, which won the Trillium Book Award for Poetry. He is also the author of numerous essays and reviews, and teaches English at Laurentian University at Georgian College.

*ACKNOWLEDGMENTS*

Poems in this book have appeared, often in altered form, in a number of anthologies and journals. My heartfelt thanks to their editors: *Barrow Street, Cincinnati Review, Crab Orchard Review, Fiddlehead, Grain, Maisonneuve, Shenandoah,* and *Zeek.* "Psalm of Scranton" was included in *The New Canon* (Véhicule Press, 2006), edited by Carmine Starnino.

I've piled up a lot of debt working on this book. So, spectacularly effusive thanks are appropriate and probably long overdue:

First, to Ken Babstock, Harold Heft, and Michael Redhill, who have been invaluable for their support and advice.

To the following friends and family for their encouragement and insight: Gil Adamson, Jason Brent, the Colloquistas, Cynthia Good, Vivé Griffith, Don McKay, Martha Sharpe, and my parents, Richard and Roberta Sol.

To the folks at Anansi, past and present, for their professionalism and enthusiasm: Martha Sharpe, Laura Repas, Matt Williams, Lynn Henry, Julie Wilson, Janie Yoon, Sarah MacLachlan, and the Grand Master, Scott Griffin.

For their help on research, anecdote, and vivid detail: the Cincinnati Bernstein clan, Jessica Lynn, Rabbi Don and Greta Lee Splansky, Felicia Sol, Eric Brown, Tony Chemero, and Cynthia Silverman.

To the Ontario Media Development Corporation, whose support of my last book helped to light my fire for this one, and to the Canada Council for the Arts and the Ontario Arts Council for financial support during the early stages.

To Helen Sol, who could have taught Jeremiah a thing or two about truth-telling.

To my boys, who give me reasons.

And to Yael, who believes.